SUM

&ANALYSIS

OF

THE

LONGEVITY

DIET

Discover the New Science Behind Stem Cell
Activation and Regeneration to Slow Aging,
Fight Disease, and Optimize Weight

A GUIDE TO THE BOOK
BY VALTER LONGO, PhD

BY ZIPREADS

NOTE: This book is a summary and analysis and is meant as a companion to, not a replacement for, the original book.
Please follow this link to purchase a copy of the original book: https://amzn.to/2NglRiW

TABLE OF CONTENTS

SYNOPSIS

In his book *The Longevity Diet: Discover the New Science Behind Stem Cell Activation and Regeneration to Slow Aging, Fight Disease, and Optimize Weight,* Dr. Valter Longo presents a wealth of research in support of both his Longevity Diet as well as his Fasting-Mimicking Diet to increase healthy longevity; fight weight gain; and treat diabetes, cancer, autoimmune disease, neurodegenerative disease, and cardiovascular disease.

Dr. Longo first introduces the reader to populations of centenarians around the world—places where an abnormally high percentage of the population lives past 100. Fascinated with these "blue zones," Longo decided to dedicate his life not just to the science of living longer, but to the science of living *healthier* longer. Through his research into blue zones in Okinawa, Japan and Molochio, Italy, among others, Longo identified many common factors in the diets and lifestyles of these populations. He spent the next twenty years testing various aspects of his research on yeast, mice, monkeys, and eventually humans to discover just how effective these diets were at increasing longevity.

What his research has found is that beyond a pescatarian, mostly plant-based diet, periods of "fasting-mimicking," or tricking your body into believing that you're fasting, can have incredibly rejuvenating effects on your cellular composition. Fasting-mimicking can not only help delay and prevent the diseases that are the most common causes of death around the world but can also help to cure and reverse diseases well into their progression.

The Longevity Diet is the culmination of more than twenty years of rigorous research, and Longo is quick to condemn the latest fad diets that claim to work miracles but offer no guarantee of long-term health benefits. While he is also quick to admit FMD and the Longevity Diet still have a long way to go in terms of large-scale studies, he believes the initial proven benefits of these diet therapies couldn't be kept silent any longer.

CHAPTER SUMMARIES & KEY TAKEAWAYS

CHAPTER 1: LONGEVITY

Dr. Longo opens the book by recounting time spent during his childhood in the small Italian town of Molochio. In 2012, Molochio had four centenarians in a population of just 2,000 people. Longo spent summers as a child in Calabria, Italy, another town where he believes the local diet is the key to the longevity of its residents. Meat was eaten just once a week and the majority of meals consisted of pasta, fish, vegetables, olive oil, and garbanzo beans. Even dessert consisted of nuts and fruit rather than sugary cakes.

We then follow Longo to his adolescence with his aunt in Chicago. He was unaware at the time of just how unhealthy the Chicagoan diet was—all sugary drinks, fried foods, cheese, milk, and meat with every meal of the day. It's something he coins "the heart attack diet."

After Chicago, Longo joined the army and moved to Texas where his diet was stuffed with meat-based proteins, fats, and sugary sodas. While he grew significant muscle mass during this period, he argues that a high-protein diet isn't the key to strength training. Rather, a low-protein, low-sugar diet interspersed with periods of normal protein does more to generate new muscle cells.

After the army, Longo went to school for music, but soon shifted his focus to science. He was fascinated by aging, by his healthy ancestors in Italy and their obese counterparts in

Chicago. He wanted to understand the connections between diet, lifestyle, health, and disease, and so he changed his major to biology. Longo contends that the current state of research arguing that aging is caused by free radicals and can be reversed with increased antioxidants is missing many pieces of the puzzle, not to mention it doesn't seem to work. He argues that we must tackle aging and longevity from a broader perspective.

CHAPTER 2: AGING AND JUVENTOLOGY

Key Takeaway: Programmed aging is the death of an individual for the better of the species.

Though a hotly contested debate with many competing theories, Longo believes that species are genetically programmed to die in order to allow for the continuation of the species as a whole. Some studies with bacteria have shown that when organisms are more concerned with their individual survival, and therefore live longer, the species will die out sooner than if the individual organism is willing to die for the next generation.

Key Takeaway: To increase human longevity, we must increase protection and repair systems.

Rather than focus on any particular disease or condition associated with aging, Longo takes a broader, philosophical approach to increasing lifespan. While there is no evolutionary benefit to living past eighty—you are already past years of procreation—he believes that with the proper genetic and dietary adjustments, we can train our bodies to live longer without harming the species as a whole. As opposed to programmed aging, he calls this programmed longevity, and it focuses on improving the body's repair systems therefore delaying parts of the aging process.

Key Takeaway: Juventology is the study of youth

A term coined by Longo himself, he argues that rather than attempt to fix small contributors to aging and death—such as an increase in free radicals or high cholesterol—we must improve the repair and regeneration systems in our bodies. If you are replacing a part in a car, for example, then fixing that part becomes unnecessary. And replacing an old part with a new one will always provide superior results to fixing the old one.

Key Takeaway: Certain genes are responsible for triggering the aging process.

Currently, the human body begins the aging process at around 40 to 50 years old. During his doctorate program, Longo was determined to find a way to expand that to 60 or 70 years. While studying the aging of yeast, Longo discovered two genes responsible for aging that were both triggered by sugar consumption. He found two other genes triggered by protein consumption. He also found that starvation was an effective method to increase longevity, albeit an unpleasant one.

Years later, Longo studied a group of people in Ecuador with a genetic mutation known as Laron syndrome. The form of dwarfism they have also seems to protect them from cancer and diabetes, even when combined with unhealthy eating habits. Longo believes their mutation in the growth hormone receptor holds the key to increased protection and regeneration necessary for increased longevity.

CHAPTER 3: RESEARCH METHODS

Gene regulation through diet can extend your healthy lifespan. However, Longo cautions against taking dietary advice from just anyone. The suggestions Longo makes are rooted in science, research, and experiment. Some combinations of foods may be healthy for an older person, but cause problems in someone younger. There are no one-size-fits-all dietary solutions, but all solutions should follow the five pillars of longevity.

Key Takeaway: All diets should be tested against the five pillars of the longevity diet.

Longo argues that many fad diets, such as Atkins or Paleo, utilize only one or two of the following five pillars. While this can mean they are effective in the short term, they are often not sustainable in the long term, and can even cause more damage than good. In fact, high-protein, high-fat, low-carb diets are actually some of the worst for your health when assessed from a multi-disciplinary point-of-view.

Basic/Juventology Research

All recommendations of Dr. Longo are rooted in science. He performs his research on yeast, mice, monkeys, and humans in order to test its efficacy in increasing longevity.

Epidemiology

This is the study of cause and effect of risk factors for health problems. If Longo and his team suspect high sugar intake leads to increased diabetes, for example, they will test that hypothesis against the general population.

Clinical Studies

Scientific hypotheses must be tested in controlled clinical studies in order to determine their legitimacy and causality. All of Longo's theories have been put to this test, though many of his sample sizes are admittedly small.

Centenarian Studies

Even once a theory passes the first three hurdles, it must be confirmed that it is safe for a lifetime of use. Longo compares his results against the health and lifestyle choices of the oldest populations on the planet.

Studies of Complex Systems

Nothing is simple, and no change in your diet will act independently of the rest of your bodily functions. Longo is sure to understand the entire picture of how each dietary recommendation may affect another system in your body.

CHAPTER 4: THE LONGEVITY DIET

Key Takeaway: Our diets consist of three main macronutrients and a variety of micronutrients.

Proteins – Generally composed of 20 amino acids which are frequently used by the body to create additional proteins and generate new muscle

Carbohydrates – There are both simple and complex carbohydrates, simple carbs trigger rapid release of insulin by the pancreas and should be avoided

Fats – Major source of energy storage in all animals; dietary fats can be saturated, monounsaturated, and polyunsaturated

Micronutrients – These are vitamins and minerals such as B12, vitamin D, and calcium that are critical to our bodies functioning. Most adults are deficient in some minerals and Longo recommends taking a multivitamin two to three times per week.

Key Takeaway: High protein and sugar consumption activates the growth hormone receptor.

This receptor—the one that was mutated in the Ecuadorian dwarves—increases insulin levels and insulin-like growth factor 1 (IGF-1), which is associated with increased prevalence of cancer and diabetes. Proteins derived from the growth hormone receptor can also trigger another set of genes responsible for aging, TOR-SK6. Yet another gene linked to aging, PKA, is linked to increased sugar consumption.

Key Takeaway: Basic Guidelines for the Longevity Diet

Follow a pescatarian diet – Limit fish to two or three portions per week; your diet should be mostly vegetables, nuts, and legumes.

Consume less protein – 0.31 to 0.36 grams of protein per pound of body weight per day. Increase this slightly after age 65. Protein should come from vegetables, nuts, and fish, not red or white meat.

Minimize bad fats and sugars – Minimize pasta, white bread, and fruit; focus on olive oil, salmon, and nuts. Longo recommends three tablespoons of olive oil per day.

Don't starve yourself outside of planned fasting – While restricting calorie intake can help your health in the short term, your body requires vitamins and minerals to function. If you follow his recommendations, you won't need to starve yourself.

Eat like your grandparents – Our bodies are products of genetic evolution over generations. As an example, Asian cultures didn't historically drink milk, and they are often lactose-intolerant.

Eat twice daily plus a snack – Unless you are underweight, you should not be eating more than three times a day. Your snack should be fewer than 100 calories and contain fewer than 5 grams of sugar. Do not skip breakfast.

Confine eating to 11-12 hours per day – If you eat breakfast at 8am, then you should finish dinner by 8pm. Do not eat anything within three to four hours of going to bed.

Practice prolonged fasting – For five days twice a year (if you're healthy), you should practice the fasting-mimicking diet. Longo addresses this plan in detail later in the book.

Key Takeaway: A low-protein, high-carbohydrate diet leads to healthy longevity.

Longo found this diet to extend the healthy lifespan of mice above all others tested. The high-protein, low-carbohydrate diets currently trending were associated with increased instances of disease and premature death, though did lead to increased weight loss in mice. Reducing protein intake can both prevent cancer as well as inhibit the growth of existing cancers.

Key Takeaway: Epidemiological studies confirmed the risks of a high-protein diet.

Longo's research found high-protein diets caused increased levels of pro-aging growth factor IGF-1, a 75 percent increase in risk of overall mortality, and a three- to fourfold increased risk in cancer mortality compared with consuming the low-protein and plant-based diet he recommends (Longo, p. 67). High animal-protein diets were also associated with increased mortality from cardiovascular disease and diabetes.

Key Takeaway: Centenarian diets around the world all share a similar structure.

Okinawa, Japan; Loma Linda, California; Calabria and Sardinia, Italy; Costa Rica, and Greece all have mostly plant-based diets that are high in fish and low in animal proteins, sugars, and saturated/trans fats. Their carbohydrates are complex and come from beans and other plants.

The unhealthy American diet consists of 29 percent meat, poultry, and eggs compared to just 3 percent for Okinawans. These differences (outlined by Longo in a helpful chart) led to much lower instances of cardiovascular disease for Okinawans compared to Americans or even other Japanese people. These findings are mirrored in all of the other "blue-zones" of longevity that Longo studied around the world.

Key Takeaway: Over age 65, increased animal-proteins can further increase longevity.

Based on his research of the centenarians of Molochio, Italy, Longo confirmed that the over-100 population had increased their animal-based foods consumption as they aged past 70 years. As levels of IGF-1 are much lower in aging populations, the risks associated with its activation are much lower as well. The increased protein intake over age 65 leads to increased muscle mass at a critical time for the aging.

CHAPTER 5: EXERCISE AND HEALTHY LONGEVITY

Physical activity is a key part of healthy longevity. All of the blue zone populations that Longo studied remained active well into old age. While there are certainly some exceptions to this rule—genetics are the strongest determinant of how long you will live—regular physical activity is a must.

Guidelines for Exercising to Increase Longevity

Walk briskly for an hour each day – This may sound like a lot of time, but perhaps you live within a couple miles of work, yet drive anyway. Maybe there is a coffee shop 15 minutes from your office you could walk to twice a day. On the weekend, walk everywhere you can, even if it's several miles each way.

Ride, run, or swim every other day – Longo recommends having an outside bike and a stationary indoor bike in case of inclement weather. He suggests 30 to 40 minutes a few times a week, plus two hours on the weekend.

Use your muscles – there are many simple tasks such as washing the dishes or mowing the lawn that humans have given over to machines or hired help. Take on as many of these as possible. And always take the stairs if you can.

Key Takeaway: Moderate to vigorous exercise decreases mortality.

Longo quotes an Australian study showing 150 minutes per week of moderate or 75 minutes of vigorous exercise led to a 47 percent reduction in mortality (p. 92). Another study of Europeans and Americans over age 62 showed a 31 percent drop in mortality for the same amount of exercise. Most of the benefit is gained in the first 2.5 hours of exercise, the incremental benefit after that is minimal.

CHAPTER 6: THE FASTING-MIMICKING DIET

While Longo had already identified that extreme calorie restriction helped the body enter a "protective state" and was an effective way to prevent disease, he also recognized the negative consequences associated with such a diet over the long term, such as a weakened immune system and unhealthy weight loss. This led him to research a way to mimic the benefits of fasting without the harmful side effects.

Testing his fasting-mimicking diet (FMD) on mice, the results were astonishing. The lifespans of the mice on the diet were expanded significantly, the mice lost abdominal fat without losing muscle mass, and the onset of cancer was pushed back from the human equivalent ages of 60 years old to 70 years old.

Key Takeaway: Periodic fasting has numerous proven health benefits.

In tests on mice, noticeable improvements were recorded in the immune system, nervous system, and pancreas. During times of fasting, damaged cells were destroyed, and stem cells were activated to replace them. After the fasting period ended, the stem cells began to regenerate the damaged organ or system. After testing in mice, Longo began testing the FMD on humans. Its goals are to switch cells into anti-aging mode, promote autophagy where cells replace their own damaged parts, kill damaged cells, and switch the body into visceral fat-burning mode.

Longo provides a chart detailing the improvements in humans adopting FMD during a controlled clinical study for five days a month for three months. Recorded benefits include weight loss, increased muscle mass, lower blood pressure, lower cholesterol (in those with high cholesterol), lower IGF-1, and lower glucose in those who were prediabetic. The frequency with which you should partake in FMD varies by body type, current health, and activity level.

Key Takeaway: All intermittent fasting is not equally healthy.

The term intermittent fasting has gained a lot of popularity in recent years, but Longo argues it is too broad for all versions of it to be considered beneficial. The real benefits of fasting only occur after two to three days of abstention from food—when the body starts burning ketones (fat) for fuel—and Longo argues any fast of this severity should be done under medical supervision. FMD was created specifically so that the average person could safely participate without the help of a doctor.

Key Takeaway: Many modern medical treatments act as band-aids rather than cures.

If a person has high cholesterol, they may be prescribed statin drugs in order to reduce the activity of an enzyme that produces excess cholesterol. Longo argues that this is simply treating a symptom rather than the disease. While statin drugs may lower cholesterol in the short term, they haven't been proven to decrease one's risk of dying. The question Longo attempts to answer is *why* that particular enzyme is overproducing cholesterol. His band-aid analogy is applicable to drugs for glucose and blood-pressure levels as well. Often, treating an individual symptom can end up causing more issues with other systems in the body.

Key Takeaway: The FMD can have serious side effects.

Longo provides a list of warnings against those for whom the fasting-mimicking diet could be harmful. These include pregnant women, people over the age of 70, those with serious illness, people who are underweight, diabetics, and those with hypertension, among others. Everyone should confer with a doctor or specialist before beginning the FMD.

Side effects can include fatigue, weakness, headaches, hunger, and slight backaches. Some of these may disappear in subsequent FMD cycles.

Key Takeaway: Day-by-day breakdown of the FMD.

*WARNING: Below is merely an overview of the fasting-mimicking diet as recommended by Dr. Longo. **DO NOT** engage in this diet program without purchasing a copy of the original book to fully understand the warnings, dangers, and ramifications of FMD. **DO NOT** engage in this diet without first consulting a healthcare professional.*

Day 1: 1,100 calories

Half calories from complex carbohydrates in vegetables, half from healthy fats and nuts along with 1 multivitamin, 1 omega-3 and omega-6 supplement, sugarless tea, and unlimited water.

Days 2–5: 800 calories

Same as day 1, but smaller portions of vegetables and healthy fats.

Day 6: Transition

Focus on vegetables, breads, pasta, fruit; minimize the consumption of meats, cheeses, and dairy.

After the FMD, return to your normal, plant-based Longevity Diet plan.

CHAPTER 7: FMD AND CANCER

Key Takeaway: Fasting before chemo could increase its efficacy and reduce side effects.

When healthy cells are starved during a fast, they go into a protective state, as we have learned from the FMD. Longo believed this protective state could be useful in chemotherapy. Since cancer cells will disregard instruction to stop growing during a fast, the body's healthy cells will have a "shield" while the cancer cells remain vulnerable. This helps to reduce the instances of side effects associated with the toxicity of chemo such as weakness, nausea, cramps, and vomiting. The starvation itself also weakens the cancer cells to begin with, making them more vulnerable to the chemo.

Though fasting for chemotherapy patients is a radical and potentially dangerous idea, Longo saw incredibly promising results during trials with mice. Clinical trials with humans are underway, and while initial results are also promising, the sample sizes are small, and the risks are not fully understood.

Longo provides a long list of warnings for anyone considering undertaking FMD during cancer treatment. FMD has not been approved as safe by the FDA for use during chemotherapy, and no one should attempt to create their own fasting program without consulting their physician or oncologist. **The guidelines for FMD during chemotherapy are different than the standard FMD and will vary by person.**

CHAPTER 8: FMD AND DIABETES

"According to the World Health Organization, the number of people diagnosed with diabetes globally has more than quadrupled in the past thirty-five years, from 100 million in 1980 to 422 million in 2014" (Longo, pp. 138-139).

Both BMI and waist circumference are high-risk factors for diabetes. For men, anything above 40 inches or a BMI over 27.5, and for women, anything over 34 inches, or a BMI over 25 can mean a six-fold increase in the risk of diabetes.

Though less discussed, protein intake may also promote diabetes.

Key Takeaway: Specific longevity recommendations for diabetics and those at risk.

Limit your eating window to 11–12 hours per day. If possible, limit it further to just 8 hours.

Eat larger portions of healthier dishes (a small amount of pasta with lots of veggies, chickpeas, and olive oil) over smaller portions of unhealthy dishes (a larger amount of pasta with cheese and sauce).

- Provides more satiety with fewer calories
- Lower insulin production
- More proteins, healthy fats, vitamins and minerals

Stick to two meals a day plus a snack. The popular notion of five or six small meals a day has been debunked. You are far more likely to exceed your recommended calorie intake this way.

Increase complex carbohydrates. Focus on whole grains, vegetables, and legumes. Remove as many sugars and starches (white bread, pasta, soft drinks) as well as saturated fats (cheese, butter, candy) as possible.

Key Takeaway: Early data in clinical trials of FMD for diabetes has shown positive results.

FMD has been shown (in limited clinical trials with fewer than 100 participants) to:

- Reduce abdominal fat

- Increase fat loss without losing muscle mass

- Kickstart cell renewal and autophagy in the pancreas to improve insulin function

WARNING: *Combining the longevity diet with the fasting-mimicking diet while taking insulin could result in hypoglycemic shock or death. If you are diabetic, DO NOT start either diet without consulting your doctor.*

CHAPTER 9: FMD AND CARDIOVASCULAR DISEASE

Cardiovascular disease represents a range of conditions including coronary heart disease, stroke, coronary heart failure, high blood pressure, and arterial disease (p. 160). Together they are responsible for one in three deaths in the United States.

Key Takeaway: Low-protein, high-healthy-fat diets are proven to reduce cardiovascular disease.

As such a widely studied condition, Longo provides numerous examples of studies around the world—in some cases spanning decades—that align with the tenets of the Longevity Diet. While the Mediterranean diet is the most similar, there are some minor differences such as cheese being far more restricted in the Longevity Diet. The Barcelona diet has a far-higher allowance for olive oil, and the Ornish diet more severely restricts all fats.

Unsurprisingly, red meat consumption has been shown to increase risk factors for cardiovascular disease, while nuts, plant-based fats, and fish have the opposite effect. Longo asserts that most studies tend to overlook the benefits of nuts and plant fats and further study is necessary.

In his own human clinical trials (limited to 100 participants) Longo found that regular FMD cycles:

- Reduced waist size

- Reduced total and LDL cholesterol

- Lowered triglycerides

- Lowered blood pressure

These effects were less prominent for healthy individuals not already at risk for cardiovascular disease. Again, as these results haven't been replicated in large-scale trials, Longo recommends consulting with your doctor or dietitian before incorporating FMD into your prevention plan.

CHAPTER 10: FMD AND ALZHEIMER'S

The primary risk factor for Alzheimer's is aging. Three of the human gene mutations associated with Alzheimer's are APP,

PS1, and tau. Longo began his tests on mice with these three mutations. Because of the late onset of Alzheimer's, Longo knew that severe calorie restriction was not a viable, long-term option in humans. Instead, he altered the diet to include a mostly normal diet but lacking in nonessential amino acids and supplemented with essential amino acids (ones that the body cannot produce on its own).

Key Takeaway: Augmented FMD cycles could reduce the risk of Alzheimer's.

While Longo does not advocate that those over age 65 practice the standard version of FMD (unless they are at severe risk for Alzheimer's), even his augmented version has shown promising results in mice. The mice alternated weekly between a normal diet and the protein-altered diet. The elderly mice saw 75 percent decreases in IGF-1. The middle-aged mice who were put on a more standard FMD plan showed noticeable cognitive improvement in old age compared to the control mice. Additionally, alternative day fasting (one day on, one day off) has also shown to improve cognitive function in mice. Human trials are yet to be completed.

Key Takeaway: Excess olive oil or nuts can improve cognitive performance.

Even if you decide not to opt for the risks of FMD in old age, Longo provides evidence that increasing olive oil or nuts in your daily diet can also provide cognitive benefits. He references the Barcelona study (*n=7,447*) once again showing the control group on a low-fat diet performed worse than both test groups for increased olive oil or nut consumption.

Key Takeaway: Coffee and coconut oil may help prevent Alzheimer's.

Longo references a study (*n=29,000*) where coffee drinkers and non-coffee drinkers showed no difference in risk of dementia. However, those who drank the most coffee had a 30 percent reduction in risk of Alzheimer's specifically (Longo, p. 184). Additionally, the medium-chain fatty acids in coconut oil are more easily converted into ketones, which may help improve cognition. No wide-scale studies on coconut oil have yet been performed and those at risk for cardiovascular disease should not take coconut oil.

WARNING: Engaging in any variation of the FMD can be very dangerous for the elderly. Those who are underweight or have low muscle mass should only consider this at the recommendation of a specialized neurologist. Any fasting cycles should be counteracted with a high-protein diet.

CHAPTER 11: FMD AND AUTOIMMUNE DISEASES

As mentioned earlier, Longo recommends you follow the diet of your ancestors as closely as possible. Many autoimmune disorders such as multiple sclerosis and Chron's disease are rooted in inflammation. This inflammation can be caused by eating foods that your body is not programmed to eat from an evolutionary perspective. Longo warns once again that large-scale studies haven't been conducted, but assures the reader there is no risk in eating the foods your grandparents ate while remaining in line with the tenets of the Longevity Diet.

Key Takeaway: FMD may replace dysfunctioning autoimmune cells with healthy cells.

In preliminary studies, FMD reduced the severity of multiple sclerosis in mice. It killed the dysfunctional cells and promoted regeneration of myelin in the spinal cord (p. 202). Additionally, the FMD seemed to promote stem cell growth, allowing the body to completely replace the autoimmune cells with healthy ones.

The small clinical trial for MS patients ($n=20$) featured a more restrictive version of the FMD with an 800-calorie transition day and just 200-350 calories of vegetables and broth daily, along with some supplements and a plant-based diet for the following six months. This same FMD cycle has been proven effective in treating Chron's disease as well with a significant reduction in symptoms. While the initial results were positive, only a single FMD cycle was tested and additional trials are needed. Longo also suggests that FMD could be beneficial in rheumatoid arthritis, though it has yet to be fully studied.

REVIEW & MEAL PLANS

Longo closes the book by recapping the tenets of the Longevity Diet along with his specific recommendations for BMI, waistline measurements, and frequency of FMD cycles based on age, health, and activity level. If you are healthy and of average weight and BMI, twice a year is all you need. If you are not healthy, your frequency should be discussed with a doctor before you begin. He also mentions the importance of personal happiness in longevity—something he realizes cannot be proven—but where anecdotal evidence abounds. Surrounding yourself with family, friends, loved ones, or a church group can help extend your life, but so can living alone indulging in your favorite foods, taking long walks, and enjoying every day. The most important factor he stresses is enjoyment.

Lastly, Longo provides a two-week meal plan for an average, healthy person aged 18 to 65. The meals are very simple, are mostly plant-based with minimal fish, and include breakfast, lunch, a snack, and dinner, though to stick to the longevity diet you must choose between lunch OR dinner, unless you are underweight. The meal planner includes recipes such as pasta with broccoli and black beans, wild rice and green beans with garlic, multiple salads, grilled eggplant, bean pasta, minestrone, and several seafood dishes. There is little to no dairy with the exception of parmesan cheese and feta, the occasional piece of dark chocolate, and all cow's milk has been replaced with nut milk or goat's milk.

The final appendix consists of nutritional guides to various sources of micronutrients such as folate, calcium, and omega-3s to help you build your own Longevity Recipes going forward.

The Longevity Diet—if it is as effective as initial trials suggest it is—could revolutionize the way we treat the diseases that most commonly afflict us in old age and which are the deadliest killers in the world. Dr. Valter Longo has spent his life researching the potential benefits of diets low in animal proteins and rich in plant-based complex carbohydrates and healthy fats. He began his work on microorganisms before moving up to mice, then monkeys, and finally to limited human trials. While he tirelessly mentions that large-scale human trials still need to be completed, the findings he presents are consistently positive and certainly encouraging for anyone suffering from one of these all-too-common afflictions.

The Longevity Diet is not just another diet book with a list of healthy foods and recipes to follow. Each chapter is overflowing with data from his own research, from clinical trials, from epidemiological studies, and anecdotal evidence as well. While the results of the research in support of the fasting-mimicking diet are undeniably promising, the consistent caveat that large-scale trials haven't yet been conducted is a glaring repetition for the reader. One can both applaud his caution and simultaneously feel concern about it. The fact that he includes no studies on any condition where the fasting-mimicking diet *didn't* prove to be effective opens the possibility for cherry picking.

The early parts of the book are filled with much of Longo's personal history and he spares no opportunity to mention he was originally studying to be a rock musician. Thankfully, his personal anecdotes diminish in frequency as the book progresses, being replaced by innumerable studies supporting each individual claim of the FMD along with the state of the science currently known about each disease's progression.

All-in-all the arguments in favor of the Longevity Diet and the Fasting-Mimicking Diet are compelling. The risks— though consistently broadcast by Longo in an attempt to dissuade readers from inventing their own FMD—are minimal if the plan is done correctly and supervised by a doctor. The benefits touted here would certainly seem to outweigh any potential risks for the average healthy person such as mild fatigue or headaches during fasting. But for any person suffering from a particular condition, it is advised not to proceed with any part of the Longevity Diet until consulting with a professional.

If you suffer from a painful or debilitating autoimmune disorder such as Chron's or MS; if you are at high risk for cancer, Alzheimer's, or cardiovascular disease; or if you're simply concerned with living the healthiest life possible, the Longevity Diet may be able to help.

BACKGROUND ON AUTHOR

Dr. Valter Longo is an Italian-American biogerontologist originally from Genoa, Italy. He is known for his studies on fasting and nutrient-response genes on cellular protection and aging. He is currently a professor of gerontology and biological science at the University of Southern California.

He received his Bachelor of Science in Biochemistry from the University of North Texas and his Ph.D. in Biochemistry from the University of California, Los Angeles. His postdoctoral research at USC focused on the neurobiology of aging and Alzheimer's disease. Longo is a founding member of USC's Biology of Aging program as well as the director of the USC Longevity Institute. In 2010, he received the Nathan Shock Lecture Award from the National Institute on Aging at the National Institute of Health (NIH). In 2013, he received the Vincent Cristofalo "Rising Star" Award in Aging Research from the American Federation for Aging Research (AFAR).

Longo founded a health supplement company, L-Nutra that provides a supplement marketed as ProLon for those partaking in the fasting-mimicking diet. This has been presented as a conflict of interest by some. Longo maintains, however, that he donates all of the proceeds both from L-Nutra and from the sale of *The Longevity Diet* towards research into longevity and other charitable organizations. *The Longevity Diet* was originally released in Italian and is his first book.

END OF BOOK SUMMARY

*If you enjoyed this **ZIP Reads** publication, we encourage you to purchase a copy of <u>the original book</u>.*

We'd also love an honest review on Amazon.com!

Made in United States
Troutdale, OR
07/01/2023

10924518R00022